necessary rebirths

a collection of poems + prose for awakening

nicole m. long

VICTORY AUETER

necessary rebirths copyright © 2019 by Nicole Long. All rights reserved. No part of this book may be used or reproduced in any matter whatsoever without written permission except in the case of reprints in the context of reviews.

Victory Aueter Publishing LLC

ISBNs:
978-0-578-57531-5 (Paperback)
978-0-578-60487-9 (Ebook)

Cover and interior design by: Dania Zafar
Cover photograph by: Jessica Felicio on Upsplash

Attention: Schools, Organizations, and Businesses
Quantity discounts with bulk purchase are available for educational, business, or sales promotional use. Contact booksales@victoryaueter.com for more information.

dedication

to the souls who find themselves
reading this book—
may you always remember that you are divine.

contents

section 1
surviving the jungle   1

seldom prayers matter none	3
trauma started early	4
ghetto proper	6
uneducated with degrees	8
guts and glory	9
on living alone	10
homies, lovers, friends	12
carnal pleasures	13
crashing and burning	14
by any other name	15
coming up for air	16
racing around the wheel	17
a lifetime of sister-friends	18
summer-time, fine	19
course correction	20
when i glance in the mirror	21
what a life	22
runny concealer	23
freedom is a birthright	24
blurry vision	25
one mistake makes two	26
they all left a void	27
holding up the wall	28
metamorphosis	30
black bitch	31
waiting for love, again	32
dancing with the devil	33
speed demons	34
land of the free	35
ties that bind	36

section 2
awakening to self   37

meet the suitor   39
the honeymoon phase   40
after the i dos   41
distance separates us   43
strange things happen sometimes   44
i belong to no one   45
meet you in the dark   46
scar tissue forms slowly   47
still in the race   48
on days that end in y   49
them feelings   50
the phoenix takes flight   51
women do what they want   52
internal realities   53
the day you meet your maker   54
everyday martyrs   55
the future is for dreamers   56
the ego's deception   57
venus in libra   58
over capacity   59
reciprocity   60
rebels yell   61
the prototype   62
a savior   63
annihilated   64
genetic composition   65
this lifetime   66
wounds need dressing   67
the time of nihilists   68
sacred beings   69
gratitude   70

section 3
integrations 71

on days like today 73
in solitude 74
greener grass 75
we're all celebrities 76
propaganda and slander 77
truth is paramount 78
harbingers of destiny 79
purgatory 80
kindness for your traumas 81
check the fineprint 82
divine feminine 83
divine masculine 84
divine love 85
god is with us 86

section 4
liberation 87

community 89
forgiving myself 90
building a legacy 91
growing with the flow 92
mirrors don't lie 93
defining love 94
design yourself 95
making friends with mortality 96
the truth about nature 97
towards the light 98
tribe 99
perspective 100
all in good time 101

lesson from my sorrow	102
at home in nature	103

section 5
ascension   105

for busy days	107
the descent teaches you	108
intimacy and me	109
keeper of self	111
work, sleep, blues	112
new realities	113
new life, same body	114
dancing under the moon	115
centuries in the making	116
dancing with you	117
one source	118
i am whole	119
go where the pin drops	120
a letter to bravehearts	121
alternate realities	122
here's your reality check	123
paradise	124
piece of peace	125
for lovers	126
conversations with god	127
the eye of the beholder	128
what life taught me	129
the world came before me	130
marriage on our terms	131
all the things we couldn't do	132
expansion	133
holy trinity	134

necessary rebirths

section 1

surviving the jungle

seldom prayers matter none

god, did your heart grow cold—
or did you turn down the volume
on my cries?

i've called for you, have you
forgotten the sound of my voice—
have you no memory of who i am?

that much time couldn't have
passed us by.

if you are up there now, tell me—
why didn't you protect me?

trauma started early

some of those formative years
are mostly a blur—tiny recollections
of things i witnessed, places i've seen—
people i knew.

community surrounded me—
a love and togetherness
with crimes from time to time.

my environment was gritty and beautiful—
where i experienced many firsts.

growing up in the inner-city of america
playing till the streetlights came on,
running through creeks, picking up frogs,
keeping up with the pack.

i wore skirts while jumping fences—
and tasted the sweet nectar from honeysuckles.

there were happy times
there were wretched times—
but i never felt like i wasn't enough.

i didn't have to believe that i needed more
my family did what they could—keeping food
on the tables, stabilizing my life, ensuring
that this ray of light had a space to fit in.

it wasn't until i met the outside world
that i ever felt like i didn't belong—

that my being wasn't enough, that i had
to fit in or be like the others to be accepted.

but add in separation and then divorce, and you'd have
the recipe for a childhood of anticipating
departures, expectations of things going wrong—
and the sullen longing for completion.

it's taken me thirty-something years to override
the trauma. and i realize now that people
come, and people go.

though any of these conditions would
make a sane person break—it makes emotional
intellects lose their shit.

so imagine what it does to impressionable youth.

ghetto proper

people turn their noses up and assume
the way we speak is broken, uncultured—unkempt.

as if the african-american vernacular english
that i speak at home isn't as prized and
american as their apple pie.

the very same words that i use with
my family, shortened—hyphenated
and enunciated with a twang that
only we can understand.

our freeness to speak as we so choose
amongst those who get our language
the inside jokes—the lingo that's made
its way onto the screens and placards in
gift-shops across the ocean blue.

the same words that bring in billions
for entities who could give a care
less about the ways of our world.

the profits—the margins,
imbalances all around.

i was told that i'd need to learn how
to speak in a way that the world would
understand—that i had to clear up my
words so that i could get a job, be respected
and thrive in this space and time.

that i, as a black woman in america,
had better learn how to switch
and code—reconfigure the way
i present my thoughts in prose if i
am to climb the ranks.

i'll have you know i've done none of the
sort. i've kept my dc-bred tongue tricks and
my guyanese kissing of the teeth for
my ghetto is next to godliness—and it deserves
to reverberate throughout the universe.

my predilection for words that are both
familiar and foreign make me exactly who
i am. a fabulous wordsmith with the juice—
and i know we'll all go down in history for
our steez.

so, i'll have you know i am fluent in
two languages—american english
happens to be one of them.

uneducated with degrees

i took up studies at a few universities—
all for those door-opening pieces of paper
emblazoned with sigils and brimming with the promise
for a network of america's finest matriculates.

so there i was, eager and excited to join the ranks
of the echelon of thinkers and doers—grabbing loans
like they were going out of style.

i was an easy target—prey for the
american dream system that falsely claimed
that to get ahead i'd have to invest
in my education—by any means
necessary.

never once knowing to check the fine print on the
repayment terms of sky-rocketing balances—
mostly interest, very little principal.

i got a few papers and a ball and chain that
threatens to snuff out all semblances
of my reality.

pages of payment histories later, and i find myself
thinking how unnecessary this debt is—
what a farce, a scheme
to which i must break free.

though i shouldn't condemn my actions,
'cause i wouldn't be right here—now would i?

guts and glory

considering what home means to me—
and it's hit or miss, and ever-changing.

i've lived in a few states, jumping from
apartment to couch—trying to find my groove.

how can anyone build up roots of their own
without allowing time for the grass to grow
underneath their feet?

then i remember what my family taught me—
and the lessons of life that i've gathered.

home is wherever i am.

on living alone

i moved to a big city the first chance i got—
running from or to something, i didn't care.

all i knew was i wanted out of this place
that held and cocooned me for as long
as i could remember.

i wanted a radical change—something
to propel me into the unadulterated
trust of self, and it worked a little too well.

i relished in my solo journey—learning
and healing, and circumventing the rules
that were handed to me.

i exclaimed with remarks—that people
who were afraid to be alone needed just that.

i took my own advice, too.
many days i'd sit with myself—loving
and appreciating who i was at that exact
place, at that exact time.

solitude was the ever-flowing endowment
from which i'd have the chance to strike it rich.

i spoiled me in ways that my budget allowed—
champagne and chips on friday nights,
jammies from box-stores, and weekend excursions
wherever the train could take me.

bold, daring and smart—i even played my
hand at being my own wing-woman,
approaching men whose beauty matched
the external and internal representation of my own.

for me, life is like school—yet the board-approved
curriculum couldn't ever teach me what my instincts
as a gal on her own in a big city did.

homies, lovers, friends

i loved a lot in this lifetime—
my cup overflowed and runneth over.

even in brevity and longevity—
i regret nothing.

carnal pleasures

look at you—
miss twenty-something.

young, wild and free—
traipsing round the world,
oysters at your fingertips.

ah, miss twenty-something
what has this life offered you—
have you ever stopped to
do more than just think?

crashing and burning

the recession hit just as i
graduated—and that big city
felt like a ghost of a town.

decimating families, destroying
economies, and pressuring folks
to consider ending their lives.

that city and its chaos sent me
and my bright ideas home,
licking my wounds—
trying to understand how
i ended up back in a place
i swore i'd never again return.

a place that felt its own
catastrophe—where the rubble
was still warm and trembling
under the feet of citizens who
were so blind-sighted by the
main-street siege that they never
saw the second smite coming.

by any other name

i visit melancholy as if
i have nowhere else to be.

reliving the past, picking
at wounds—the bloody
mementos from times when
i knew better and moments
when i didn't—all the same.

how long will i remain in this
dark room whittling and crying—
unable to cope with the pain and
the trauma from mangled dreams?

coming up for air

bouncing back from a dream deferred
does some things to your psyche.

that interval teaches you a resilience
for bending without breaking—it shows
you how to block and how to take a punch.

all hail the people who get back up after
having their assess handed to them—the ones
who forgo their pride, and do what they
must to keep up the forward movement.

those who take rejection as they would praise
because they understand that adaptability
cannot wash away one's central core.

these delays, mistrials, and setbacks we face
are a recalibration—the fine-tuning of landmarks
and posts that let us know we're exactly
where we are supposed to be.

it's only when we open our eyes
and take a deep inhalation that we observe
the truth behind the emotions.

and i like what i see.

racing around the wheel

i found myself hopping from job to job
conflicted by the experiences, yet staying
for the necessity of money.

attempting to bloom where i was planted
like my grannie told me and understanding
the balance in sacrifice like my grampie showed me.

how many things did i do just to pay the bills—
missing out on joyous occasions because the
first of the month was nigh?

paying obligees before i even saved
a morsel for myself—what a rickety
dais on which i've chosen to make a career.

a lifetime of sister-friends

we are each other's mirror—revealing a truth
that is so neatly packed underneath pounds
of soil that our foundation couldn't give
way to anything new.

i suppose i should tell you that i do not always
swallow comfortably that truth—and on more
than one occasion, i've been the hypocrite, too.

yet, i suppose my sisters would tell you that to
know me is to warmly yield to the fact that people
do indeed change their minds all the time.

this growth, this maturation comes from exploration—
taking time to feel the bare bones veracity of isolation
and separation, and accepting the splits of
circumstances.

this growth comes on the heels of craving those
simpler times when the only things keeping us up
at night were our wild antics and conversations—
not babies, spouses, and considerations of bills due.

i miss my sisters—and i welcome the warm tears
following that admission. time skipped over us—
we skipped over us, leaving conversations where
they last stood, plans unfinished and check-ins missed.

sisters whose warm hugs shatter the burdens of
this women's work. sisters whose conversations
pick right back up where they left off.

summer-time, fine

love comes dressed as a familiar
stranger right as you've gotten
back into your groove—ready for
the world, and tightening
up your plans.

a stranger that asks nothing more
from you than the chance to get to know you—
as friends first because, yes, your dream
still awaits.

course correction

i didn't give up finding my way back
to that big city—i bent myself over like
an acrobat trying to make my will be
the reality that met my gaze.

i felt stronger than before—
maintaining an edge, working
these muscles so i'd be ready
when the coached called me in.

that day never came—so i built
my own way.

when i glance in the mirror

your mask shields you from the world—
but it couldn't ever block you from me.

i know the life you had to put on—
the hits and blows of which you've
borne the brunt.

how could i ever forget all that
we've been through?

what a life

how does one become
so preoccupied with life
they forget to stop and
smell the roses?

when do they forget the taste
of happiness, blood rushing
through their veins—heart
pulsating at the center?

when does one lose the joy
in their laughter?

once they move away from
the subtle moment of now.

runny concealer

there isn't enough money—
nothing, no man,
can fill your cup.

say those words aloud—
feel their vibration wrap
around your soul.

you are simply enough—
just as you are, and whatever
comes your way is just a cherry
on top of your chocolatiest
of sundaes.

breathe—can you?
allow your mask to dissolve.

let the lies you've heard break
way from your armor—let yourself
move past the fear of going crazy
to see you are not losing your mind.

you're merely getting free.

freedom is a birthright

i feel each word they uttered—
dormant on my soul trying to
take up permanent residence.

they broke me—yet, i managed
to walk away intact.

ain't no use in crying over that which
has passed—just like there's no use
in begging someone to stay after they've
chosen to go on without you.

so i'll call this opportunity
what i know it is—a blank slate,
a journey—a lot of fucking karma.

blurry vision

sticky situations are
my favorite type of party.

where the band plays through
the noise ordinance, and
the weed makes its rounds 'til 3.

you should expect nothing less
from the daring one who walks
among wild women freely.

i've always done as i'd
wished—not really thinking
about the consequences yet
trusting the divine to always
carry me through.

one mistake makes two

i've outdone myself this time
creating a life like the fables
and deciding it suits me no more.

i trimmed and snipped things
out of my life so long that—
i'm afraid of what little remains.

but i'm clear on my path—getting
back to what's pure and true.

even if that means wiggling through
tight passages towards my salvation.

even if that means going alone.

they all left a void

can you spot them—
the lessons in the partners
who claimed they loved you?

each a void—littered with
remnants of happier times.

can you feel the wind breezing
by that gaping hole in the middle
of your chest?

wafting over the grave and hollow
wounds where you've anchored
yourself with ease.

the pain, the heartache
it's all you've ever known.

how could you give that
away for whatever unknown
lies ahead?

holding up the wall

here i am self-sabotaging—
as per usual.

though i'd be lying
if i bigged-up my chest—
or appeared at home with courage.

i've gotten by for so long
pushed for so long—
cried for so long that
i wouldn't know happiness
if it was staring me in the face.

and there it is, looking at me
smiling—summoning me for a dance.

whispering to me words of healing
and chances to mend what's broken.

i thought about it for a while—
mentally checking off lists
and putting back the throwaways
just in case i need them in the future.

i hesitated right as our hands touched—
happiness and i.

i say i want to dance—but my body tenses.

what if i like how broken, how tarnished
how imperfect my world is?

what if i enjoy the struggle—because
at least i know what to expect from it?

happiness is the wild, wild west
of possibilities and i don't know what
i would even do there.

what would i play, what would i sing—
where would i live?

so i'll just move slowly to the rhythm
barely keeping the tempo.

scared to let my body be at ease
in the embrace of happiness—
but at least i'm dancing.

metamorphosis

decay doesn't happen all at once—
no, that would be too easy.

like waking up and finding out
you won the jackpot.

how else would you gain experience—
or account for years of practice
if there were no insipid process to endure?

how could you stand tall—
prepared for battle if you didn't take
a couple scuffles and falls?

how could you know yourself
if you've never run to the arms
of everyone else, first?

so you see, the pain, the pleasure,
and everything in between has
prepared you for this moment
where you've realized that it's all been
for your best and highest good—
every single part of it.

black bitch

they say i was born a sinner, so
here i am—bruised and berated
in a country that neither wants me
nor can stand as tall—as boisterous
as it does without me.

to them, i am neither muse nor saint
just a means to whatever end they choose.

their books don't carry my name
nor do they tell of my cures, my love
my strength—my devotion.

i am the sore thumb in their world—
oh—but what they wouldn't do
to get just one taste of me.

waiting for love, again

i've stopped counting the time since you left
but like the old school lover that i am—
i pine for your touch—craving your smell
dreaming of the day when we're together again.

so where are you, beloved?

last i heard, you were making your way
around the town—doing as you wish.

i suppose that's alright—no one likes
a jealous lover, not even me.

so i'll see you later—i've got enough of life
going to keep me occupied, contented
and full until you make your way back
home to me.

dancing with the devil

we've all been there—
go 'head, tell the truth.

a flash of a thought hinting
at your desire for something more.

what spirits are on the other side
guiding, nudging—helping you
to not fuck it all up for a
second or two of quick appeasement?

speed demons

sometimes i feel worthless—
like everyone gets ahead except me.

as if i am spinning my wheels
not quite getting beyond the 60 mph hump.

so busy watching my speed—comparing
velocities that i missed my blasted exit.

rode straight past my turn,
shifting to the next gear.

when will i learn to cease keeping up
with strangers?

land of the free

dear god,
that world that
you made—my guy,
it's fucking brutal.

have you seen what
they've done with
the place?

ties that bind

lookin' at my life and
the agreements made
under duress.

somehow i'm ballsy
enough to say i don't
want or need them anymore.

or—if i'm honest, i'd retort
that i've been ready to burn
it all down—leave all this shit
right where it currently stands.

that i'd leave it all frozen
in time, aloof to the moment
when i'd again return.

if i'm honest, i'd tell you that i am
ready to find out who i really am—
to see why they've worked so hard
to keep me unlettered and in the dark.

ignorant to my greatness and the
universe of possibilities that entails.

well, if i'm honest, i'd tell you i have
been cut those ties, and what you see
now is only what remains of me.

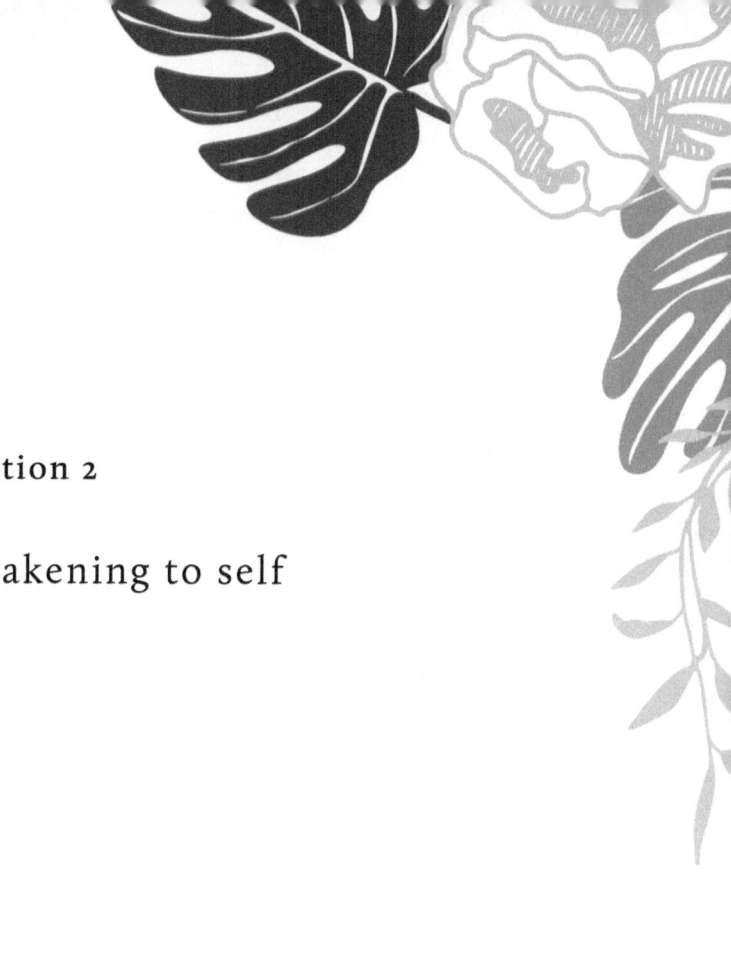

section 2

awakening to self

meet the suitor

you asked to pour into me
i smiled—romanticizing the idea.

what a noble, grand gesture
even for a hopeless romantic like me.

the honeymoon phase

everything's great—until it's not.

after the i dos

this is the part they never show you—
not in magazines or the evening news.

the ever after, happily.
the mundane, the predictable—
albeit, an enjoyable routine.

what a simple, beautiful life.

but what happens when the bride
and the groom want it no more?

when the rumblings underneath
become unsettled longings to
blow up the picture that sits
atop the fireplace mantle?

what if i said we're ringing in
around a 7 on the richter scale?

not bad, by the least—
but certainly room for more.

imagine if i said that being
married is lukewarm and hot—
that on some days i like it more
than i love it.

or how responsibilities usurp my energy
dimming me to a whisper of
who i once was?

look at me—
ungrateful, unsteady
all with carats and a picket fence.

i see why all the best movies
end it after the highlight of walking
down the aisle—because the rest
of the reel is so raw.

distance separates us

i used to run up and hug my momma
laugh and play with my dad—feud
with my sisters and brothers.

but before i knew it, we were
dispersed around the eastern coast—
leaping in faith and starting over.

i'm not sad about it anymore,
it means nothing other than
we aren't physically present with
each other—the love we have
remains the same.

i know life was supposed to
unfold this way, so is it the
memory of the past that
makes me still a little sad
at the realization that nothing is
the same?

strange things happen sometimes

how are you here—
in this life, in this town
cast in a mold that was
tailor-made for someone else?

if you were to stop
and feel—and do, and be
you'd realize that the only
person you ever needed was
standing in your shoes already.

i belong to no one

wife, daughter—
just a few names
that ring true.

these are the badges—
chosen and worn
with honor.

though i never really
stopped to think of
what i wanted to be called—
the names, the tasks that would
take me where i wanted
or needed to go.

if i did recollect my desires,
would they tell the same story
to me?

meet you in the dark

oh, good girl—
show me your bad side.

i want to feel
what you can do.

scar tissue forms slowly

picking my wounds again and again—
watching as blood spills out
as if it's waited for eons,
imagining a release like this.

its unfurling of pain now
covers me head to toe—imprints
as reminders of every place i've been,
every stone i've turned and every
bridge i've burned.

still in the race

all that looking, searching,
making do just to get by.

even after i saw that
i didn't have to no more.

what am i aiming for
waiting for, working for—still?

on days that end in y

monday to sunday—
i'm mastering the art
of dodging detonations.

learning to relinquish the
custody of all the things
that once passed me by.

what's meant for me is
here for me—no if, ands
or buts in between.

them feelings

i'm a human—not a machine
i felt what scared me—
for god's sake
i experienced it all
so i was clear on
what to do next.

it's true what they say—
experience makes for
the best teacher, so why
would i change anything
about my life?

the path that led me
through the fire is
the same one that
brought me to the rain.

the phoenix takes flight

with this fire in my soul—
i face the light of day
wings spread, eyes open
and soaring past the atmosphere.

this world has more
to offer than i was
first led to believe—
and now, my purpose is to
live within that wisdom,
thrive within that truth.

go as far as my two wings
will take me.

women do what they want

when did i become so dull—
have i forgotten what makes
me, me?

so rigid and serious—
when that's not all i was
born to be?

internal realities

what would it take for
me to embody what
i feel on the inside—
permanently, consistently
and happily?

will it require me throwing
out my whole life—
pressing restart on the console?

life isn't always as dramatic
as a blank slate—sometimes
there's no opera singer belting
out the recitative to my inner
dialogue as i stroll down city streets.

most of this journey is me—
alone in purgatory with
my creations, undergoing
the arduous task of closing
out chapters, one book at a time.

i had no idea i'd left this much
of my life untouched—this much
of my work undone.

this much of my heart unclassified.

who knew you needed so little to survive?

the day you meet your maker

you can't stop the inevitable
unfolding of your life.

so go with the flow or stand
proudly—change is the only constant.

the single thread that becomes your
ego's undoing is called accountability.

be shocked if you must—
aghast, perplexed.

i know—
it's a damning feeling
when you see you're the one
holding the strings.

everyday martyrs

i've depleted my resources—
pouring in to their cups
while i sit parched.

who taught me to hate
myself this way?

was it the years of programming
and the habits i picked up
just 'cause they felt right
and seemed to work
for everyone else?

or was it the pain of seeing so
many of the people i love needing
to do the same?

the future is for dreamers

i survived the madness—
and gave myself a round
of applause, for i was the
one that got free.

i flew as far as i could,
as high as i could
until i couldn't do it alone.

so where is my dream team?

the ego's deception

there is never enough—
of one thing or another.

wear this to stand out,
say this to feel loved.

fill his voids—forget
about your own.

venus in libra

i wanted the stability—
and i wanted something new.

a thing that held my hands and
listened to old love songs.

something that showed me
those romance flicks were right.

but life has shown me that fairytales
are a tool of oppression—that real love
takes work and disagreements can come
together for a greater good.

life has shown me that happy endings are
yours for the making if your pursuit is
sublime and you stay through the fun of the night.

over capacity

the bags of shit you tried
bringing with you—
what a heavy burden they were.

i'm glad you placed them at
the door before closing—
you know they weren't meant
to come with you this far.

reciprocity

no one asks you
how it feels when
you choose yourself—
nor do they inquire about the
way you breathe differently
without the weight of the
world on your shoulders.

so i'll ask you, how's it feel
to be free?

rebels yell

i'd get it if you didn't know
what to make of me—
the change in my rhythms
and movements.

either i'm all the way crazy
or damn-well sane—there's
a fragile line between the two.

i haven't lost my marbles—
my purpose of being is pristine.

so if my actions or words
are offensive to you, perhaps
we're playing for different teams.

the prototype

our blueprints, they're different
and coded with intricate data.

an unfolding of stories and lifetimes
of gifts and trauma all packed within
that helix of a form.

the way i flow, the way i breathe
it's all specific to me.

no carbon copy—no screenshot
can replicate what's within.

a savior

everything you want and need
exists already—within you.

annihilated

here i am simply unable to
dream of the morning
after—once i've heard the tales
of my own demise.

ingesting their poisoned mana
one syllable, one inflection at a time.

i got caught in the chasm
of polarities, overpowered
the homeostasis that dwells within.

now—what do i do?
where do i begin?

genetic composition

a spirit that's been gathered.
bio-dust—not just the physical matter.

from the galaxies afar—greeting you,
loving you in real time.

though i am more than just a checkbox
i dare not exclaim the dash-american, either.

everything they threw at me and everything that
stuck is merely the construction of a construct.

something to assist them in keeping up with human
inventory. so why wouldn't these brainwaves
need rewiring—a new cadence from which to grow?

this lifetime

i'm feeling myself
this time around.

like there's no mountain
i cannot climb—no ocean
too rough for safe travels.

the bumps in the road taught me
gravity—and the split-second
choices revealed the warrior and legionary.

wounds need dressing

pain can singe your heart
close you up, shut you down—
once it's nestled in your
crown or tissue.

confess the agony it brings you
the highs, the lows, the in betweens—
the medicine is in the clearing
let love protect and imbue.

the time of nihilists

they set for us the standards—
right and wrong, and tolerant.

but the mores we follow—
are they just because.

who decides the honoring?

sacred beings

the ways of the world—
leave it all in ruins.

you're the catalyst for
a new normal—how
else will the world
witness what is possible
if you don't use your head start?

gratitude

thank the all that is for your life
and everything that's
ushered you to the place
of weightless.

thank yourself for the courage
that powered you in
standing tall, sitting even
to rest those muscles from
that white-knuckle grip of
needing to control.

with your eyes opened or closed
you have the providence to see
this moment as it is.

with your form you can feel
the energy that's taken on the physical
and that which is still searching.

with your words you channel a force
that's greater than you, making sense
out of the dysfunction.

give your undivided attention
to the present. deliver on those
promises made to younger you.

and while you're at it, re-write yourself
a new story with all the chapters you can dream.

section 3

integrations

on days like today

i set alarms to remind me of
all i'm responsible for.

the dishes that have piled up
my hair that needs dressing—
the food that should be in
my stomach but still sits
somewhere in a market aisle.

there's a part of me that
ignores the instructions—
swiping and shutting off
their blaring screech.

these days, i prefer to let
the present be all that matters to me—
letting me be all that matters.

then, i remember about balance
and the necessity of taking action.

the emotions, the intellect
the intentions—the yes, the no,
the and.

in solitude

submerged in salt water—
eyes closed, mind free.

time stands still—
i am whole, at peace.

greener grass

emotions you smile through—
parts that leave you seething.

feel *those* feelings, let them
teach you about you.

we're all celebrities

staged photos—
contorted and distorted
for a double-tap.

fun in-scroll—
befitting for real life.

must we pretend
everything is gilded—
put-together all the time?

propaganda and slander

breaking news flashes before us
disproportionate fodder in the
name of the founders.

layers of half-truths
immortalized on surfaces
as we verge on a future that
seems bleak.

how will citizens survive a world of
insanity never once asking who
does their safe keep?

truth is paramount

look through the frame
they made for you.

you're no caged animal
nor nigger by name.

you're simply a divine being—
and you belong right here.

harbingers of destiny

i stepped out on faith—
the same as you've done before.

unknowing all that could happen—
but what a beautiful life thus far.

with all i've been given—
the trials, the blessings, the lessons.

why do i still fear the future
when my path was already written?

purgatory

you're too far gone to stop now—
much closer to your dreams
than you are to their reality.

so don't stop here—keep your
footing, your heart is in the right
place, though the chaos of your mind
can consume you—squarely
like the rapture that it is.

kindness for your traumas

i thought of you the other day.

i winced, i cried—
i let you go.

check the fineprint

i prefer harmony and balance,
taking the unfavorable when required
but also knowing that sometimes
shit just happens.

moving forward slowly is
still traction as long as
you're aware of your surroundings.

creating your reality is no small business
because nothing is everything,
and everything means nothing at all.

as trivial as it may seem in these words
we're all one—connected at the root
in spite of our vast and sometimes
ghastly differences.

so cursing you is still cursing
me, giving to you is still giving to me.

how are we not pouring in to each
other if we're truly apart of the same family?

divine feminine

now i see it so clearly—
the voids i thought their
absence would leave.

how foolish i was
unable to see that i am
the entirety of the universe—
and they couldn't live without me.

divine masculine

we all have it in us—
the practical, the by
any-means-necessary
fire in our bellies that give us
the energy we need to strike
for gold on our first, second,
and third shots.

divine love

my love we'd never
fail at anything—
no, not even if we tried.

god is with us

we never lost our connections—
it is just sullied and buried
underneath years of muck
and dogma that keeps us
chasing our own tails.

kill your religions for this
momentous occasion—open
your eyes and mind to other
possibilities that maybe you
are wrong, perhaps you've been
duped, and maybe—just maybe
the savior you're waiting for is not
some entity outside of yourself.

not some god whose remarkable
actions shifted the planes of space
and time.

maybe all along the saving grace
was you—yes, you.

is that really hard to believe
that you are capable—
or that you don't
even need saving—that you are
as powerful as the guardians
and divinely anointed victors
from storybook lands?

take back your authority will you—they need
you more than you ever needed them.

section 4

liberation

community

they can change the way you look,
give us high-rises and coffeeshops
while pushing out the lifeblood
that gave pulse to the cities.

they may take away the
landmarks, add in a juice bar
and hipster dives.

they still rob the people of their land
mark it up, flip it, and sell it back at a premium.

but what about the normal folks—
what about the dwellers, the makers and
doers—where do they get to call home?

forgiving myself

chasing closure
used to thrill me—
had me believing
that maybe, just maybe
clearer heads and a break
in time could move life
forward.

certainly not together—
we don't remember the
past for a reason.

but for a sly chance to speak
some truth and carry with us
the good—while contemplating
new beginnings since you don't
always get clean endings.

i am making peace with these
unfinished stories; leaving the
book right side up for someone
else to decide if it will be their
trash, too, or a found treasure.

building a legacy

what will you make of it—
your time on this plane?

what will you leave behind—
if anything, for those who
come next?

growing with the flow

embrace your stretchmarks—
the battle scars, the wounds.

they're proof
you've done some livin'.

mirrors don't lie

you're beautiful as is—
no enhancements,
no reductions of any sorts.

you are perfect—
just the way you are.

defining love

i didn't know what love was—
there, i said it.

i believed it was topical—
i subscribed to their definitions
thinking i could hold love in my
bare hands one day.

never once did i stop and think
of the surrender, the acceptance—
the just letting things be.

or the warmth i'd feel when
every good thing i'd ever given
was returned back home to me.

design yourself

know yourself—
you are a conduit
for energy.

you have the power
to effect change.

making friends with mortality

blooming
and withering—
like dust you'll too
merge with the wind.

so why do you stay stagnant—
stand still, stay put?

is it your fear that keeps you
where you are?

unable to enjoy the passage
of time—clinging to
things and mourning their
deaths as transformations?

no, you don't enjoy life by
staying stuck—
you soak up its goodness
moment by moment—
beginning again and again—
and again.

until you can begin again
no more.

the truth about nature

nature requires nothing from us—
it simply does as it was created to do.

it neither bends nor bucks to the paths
we've laid bare, acquiescing it does not
to our pleasures for a picturesque day.

nature doesn't give a shit about beach
houses near calabasas, it simply does
as it was created to do.

so how about you?

towards the light

sweet peace—
why run in its
opposite direction?

opting for hits to
your chakras—
explosions erupting
anytime.

life musn't be hard
all the time, give tranquility
a chance to console you—
let a new thing mold you.

presently, present be.

tribe

authenticity glares
at us more than
a time or two.

we see past the veneers,
objective in stance—
honorable in charge.

an internal compass
guides us—sustaining
and building, ebbing and flowing—
all with the ocean's tide.

there we are—
opening up our gifts
for the whole world to see.

feeling the feels—
knowing what's real.

a beautiful and
miraculous thing.

perspective

appreciate the gift
that is your life.

it is neither promised
nor is it guaranteed to be fast.

with each breath you take
you can choose to make it
as meaningful, as full—
or as empty as you'd like.

your choice may not be
the choice for me—
but it better had been the
one you damn-well pleased.

all in good time

the truth reveals
to you what you are
prepared to handle—
what you are poised to act
upon, what dragon you're
ready to slay.

lesson from my sorrow

no one could pray the pain away for me
this route was mine all my own to take.

i've found myself laid strewn on the floor
crying my tattered soul out and putting back
in its place the breath of new beginnings.

i've laughed till my heart was contented and
on the verge of exploding. i've been stabbed
in the front by people who look, speak, and
act like me.

no one could pray for the second coming for me,
though good riddances and benedictions
came as balms just when i was about to
give it all up—talk about divine timing.

knowing the power of intention and manifesting
a route that was all my own to take—
i've gathered the voids, melded them into one
and spoke life over my capacity to feel something
better, something more alive.

no one could pray the pain away for me—
i had to lose myself in the meadows of my
subconscious mind to find its hidden key.

at home in nature

i used to lace up my kicks—
buying rewards for
a week's worth of hell.

now—i exclaim at the
presence of nature
the ocean, the forest
it doesn't seem to
matter where.

perhaps for me
these places are heaven.

perhaps for me, i've tasted
the truth and don't need
no substitutes.

section 5

ascension

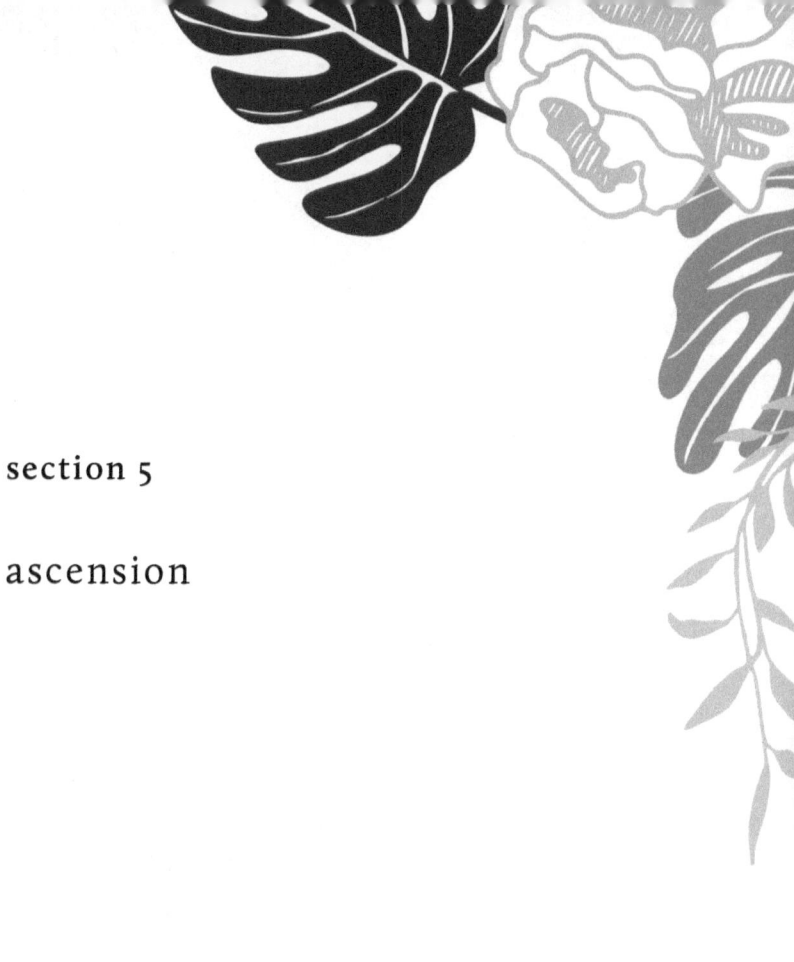

for busy days

when things get heavy,
when you're feeling like
a lot is on your mind.

before you go over the edge
remember to stop, slow down—
and breathe.

all you have is now.

the descent teaches you

most people can admit
there is something that
makes them tick when looking
in the mirror.

each one of us grapples with
something—a condition for
disharmony that's embedded
deep within us.

we do not intend to be at war
with ourselves—no, we'd never
knowingly wreak the havoc of a
million plagues on to the particles
that make up our existence.

so life teaches us to have compassion—
to hold space for ourselves, to accept who
we are, as is, no matter who says otherwise.

life teaches us to love ourselves
through solitude and uncomfortable
growth spurts that show us what it means
to be whole.

when we can observe the signs
of our soul doing the best that it can
in the moment that it's in, we learn
the beauty of simplicity—the art
of being conscious, the art of being
in tune with the universe.

intimacy and me

i once believed that i feared intimacy—
that somehow i was afflicted with
an incapacity of getting close to others.

years of sabotaging relationships
filled with my expectations and
the anticipation of chaos.

i think i wanted the disappointment
to prove to myself that my safeguards
were necessary all along.

i expected people to leave—
to get fed up with who i was,
and decide that they had
better get moving if they'd want to
salvage whatever dignity remained.

i walked alone, knowing that i could
only try but so much before the inevitable exit—
the painful routine of losing someone
again and again—and again.

it took years for me to realize
that the only person i hadn't
communed with was myself.

i'd spend so much time trying to figure
out if they were good, if i could do something
to make them happy.

how could i witness my life
through such rose-colored frames—
without needing a spectacle change?

i looked for words to convey what i felt
willing to meet people just close enough
to allow for an escape route if needed.

yes—one day i learned that this
consummate lover indeed had
commitment issues.

that i had problems staying put
and fighting for what i love because
i've only seen love walk away.

keeper of self

i thought i could
change the world and that if
i screamed loud enough
people would care.

i had it partly right—
actions are more valuable
than words—yet words
are binding agreements.

carrying something more
potent than what is seen with
your naked eye.

a surge that can only be felt,
understood, and remembered.

going silent and moving inward—
expands your comprehension
and it gives you the courage to be
the change you want to see.

work, sleep, blues

does everyone wrestle
with their bodies—
when the alarm clock
nears the danger zone?

or are they enjoying
the opportunity to rise
and do whatever thou wilt?

we're all meant to rejoice in
this life we've been given.

are you wise enough to
celebrate in yours?

new realities

old patterns are catalysts for growth
so be comfortable in the unknown
of your subconscious mind.

you're choosing where
to go from here, and the sky
is no longer a limit.

new life, same body

sleep was a welcomed reprieve
from the hell i created.

until i learned how to dream
with eyes wide open.

dancing under the moon

the air is calmer—cooler
because of you.

rest is pleasant—and
divinely guided for us, too.

how could i ever repay
you for the ways
you've helped me
repair my soul?

centuries in the making

in other relationships, i got lost—
snuggled closely to them
and their identities.

but with you it's different.

my love—
you broke the mold.

dancing with you

somehow we've made
it through the songs and
storms of life—pausing
for twirls and dipping
with the spins.

how did we find
our way to each other?

the crescendo of our love
hasn't skipped a beat since.

one source

write, sing a song—
and you'll feel me in
your laughter.

and if you look closely
you'll see me—as you
see yourself.

there is no disconnection
between you and i—
never has been, nor will
it ever be so.

i am whole

don't take it personal
if i seem distant—
i'm just enjoying this
time alone with me
myself, and i.

go where the pin drops

i travel to make a new place home—
even if only for a quick jaunt.

some location where i can get my juices
flowing, yet anchored and oriented enough
to experience what the world has to teach me.

some may say it's a luxury to travel
and in some instances, this is the truth.

but i've learned to appreciate the experiences
that come with exploring my hometown just
as much as being in a place where only
a few people know my name, and i'm unfamiliarly
versed in its sights and sounds.

a letter to bravehearts

this world can make you
second-guess yourself—
wonder if you're the only
one who thinks like you,
lives like you, loves like you.

at times it's isolating—standing
out even when you want to just fit in.

for the sake of your soul, don't ever
just fit in. there's no box big enough
to hold you—you shine, even when
you're not trying.

be proud of that—rest assured that you
are not here by accident.

so blaze your own trail, show those who
watch your moves what else is possible when
you dare to just be yourself.

alternate realities

somewhere in the galaxy is
a different version of me—
someone who didn't back down
from a fight, didn't up and move to
a different city—someone
who didn't bet on herself
every chance that she was
presented with.

i sit and think about us both—
mostly the sacrifices that made
decisions possible, and the fears
and joys surrounding me now.

here's your reality check

every part of you is
moving—down
to your very own
words and thoughts,
the so called
good and the bad.

what are you
responsible
for emitting
into the world?

paradise

i know a few places
where the sun rises from
the doorstep of mountains
and the breeze and trees
sway to the beat of heaven's drum.

the waters, they shine—
with a cerulean hue.

i will meet you there when
the night falls, when others
reach for slumber.

i will meet you there when
the world stops turning and
all the things are said—
and all the tasks are done.

piece of peace

silence has a way of
teaching you, guiding you
prepping you—for the
life and love of your dreams.

your only responsibility
is to have the capacity to receive.

for lovers

sleeping in—
going out.

i don't care what
we do—as long as
i'm with you.

conversations with god

sometimes i don't
have all the answers—
and still want
reassurance that i'm ok
and on the right path.

that's when i sit down
close my eyes, and open
my heart to speak directly
with the divine.

a practice that hasn't failed
me yet.

the eye of the beholder

when you accept your
place as artist and architect
you find yourself surrounded
by the beautiful mundane—
the extraordinary, basic building
blocks of life.

find satisfaction with your
blank canvas—it's ripe and
it's ready for you to leave
your mark.

what life taught me

duality reveals the truth for me
that i am both lightness and darkness
healed and healing—i accepted
and moved on from this truth.

there's no reason in denying
that i can be all things at any
given time, both a masterpiece
and a work in progress.

there are no mistakes on my path—
only opportunities to evolve.

to set new intentions and let life
blossom accordingly.

to remember just how far i've come
how many hurdles and pains i've
endured that haven't killed me yet.

i'm still standing, and happy—
still standing, and thriving.

and so are you.

the world came before me

drowning out my own knowing
with their thoughts, beliefs, intentions.

the discord comes from personalizing
this experience—exacting justice and
evenness for my own good.

is it possible to believe in karma,
success and justice without your hands
having to do the work?

marriage on our terms

we bonded over hip-hop—
those verses, them bumpin' beats.
a kinship, a friendship where
roots run deep.
passionate love and battle,
i'm grateful to have met another me.

blending fun with the inevitability of
maintaining; dabbling expertise with
strikes of questions like what in the
world are we doing, and how did we
make it this far?

in truth, we coast by so often that
inertia grabs hold; and we challenge
its comfortability.

not for chaos-creatin's sake, but for
our hearts in the present time.

i don't dream of happily ever afters
for i know now that to be awake with you,
eyes locked with you, is to witness eternity
unfold before us.

when you say my name, i feel you—
loving, caring, sincerely.

these years together have been
one heck of a teacher—and i'm glad
we haven't been keeping up with the score.

all the things we couldn't do

it's bout time we receive something
other than sloppy seconds—
half-assed equality
from another man's dreams.

why settle for living in their reality
when we're strong enough to
make our own?

expansion

your spirit's too big
to only sit inside
your human shell.

so why conform to
such dimensions?

holy trinity

beautiful, black woman—
hidden, forgotten, awakened.

surviving, failing—but always
succeeding in spirit.

there's no need to curse the chaos
instead, count it all joy.

second comings are a rarity—
especially when you are expecting it
vis-à-vis patriarchal meat suits.

but you, fine as wine, are the golden
child—the light and the truth we've
prayed for, the monarch of destiny
that we aimed for.

you can create our better tomorrow
since everything in this universe is
working with you.

take charge of the mothership—
your sisters are already here,
and we welcome you home.

acknowledgements

This book is a lifetime in the making, and it wouldn't have been possible without the divine being that we have termed God—or what I like to call the "all that is." I've learned that giving a name to something takes away its power—so I'll leave you with this. I am all that I am because it existed first.

Throughout my life, I've received enough guidance, love, and support to get me to a state of balance and understanding of life and its divine orders. And I'd be remiss if I didn't shout out the ones who've helped me along the way.

To my parents, the elders, and ancestors. Thank you for your prayers of protection, fights for freedom, strength, and love. Your energy covers me in the darkest of nights, and for you, I am forever grateful.

To my siblings and cousins, we have been blessed with a bond that is unshakable though we fight like oil and vinegar. Together we are powerful—together, we are more than enough.

To my loving and supportive husband, there are few words to match the gratitude in my heart for all that we've built together. I adore you, sir.

To my large and blended family—and the countless other team members, collaborators, friends, supporters, readers, and the world. Thank you for showing me what it means to love unconditionally, show up bravely, and work together for the greater good. May peace be with us all.

about the author

Nicole M. Long is a poet, writer and creative who has learned to enjoy life and all that it has to offer.

Artistically, she continues to hone her voice through spoken and written forms, visualizations, and other mediums.

Professionally, she's amassed ten years of experience in strategic services for small-to-large businesses + organizations, including content creation, authentic storytelling, video production, public relations, community relations, brand management, and digital marketing.

Today, Nicole spends her time traveling, writing, creating, and collaborating with individuals and community organizations to harness the transformative powers of art, communications, and wellness to heal and disrupt the status quo.

In her free time, Nicole enjoys gardening, cooking, traveling, and the presence of great conversations and company. Learn more about Nicole's work at www.nicole-long.com.

Photo Credit: Kimberly M. Smith

www.ingramcontent.com/pod-product-compliance
Lightning Source LLC
Chambersburg PA
CBHW021954290426
44108CB00012B/1063